NAME OF LOOK _____

EVENING ⭕

DAYTIME ⭕

FACE

MOISTURIZER

_____

CONCEALER

_____

FOUNDATION

_____

HIGHLIGHT/BLUSH

_____

EYES

BROWS

_____

EYELID

_____

LINER

_____

CREASE

_____

MASCARA

_____

LIPS

LINER

_____

LIP COLOR

_____

GLOSS

_____

NOTES

Name of Look _____

Evening ⭕

Daytime ⭕

Face

Moisturizer

_____

Concealer

_____

Foundation

_____

Highlight/Blush

_____

Eyes

Brows

_____

Eyelid

_____

Liner

_____

Crease

_____

Mascara

_____

Lips

Liner

_____

Lip Color

_____

Gloss

Notes

NAME OF LOOK _____

EVENING ◯

DAYTIME ◯

FACE

MOISTURIZER

_____

CONCEALER

_____

FOUNDATION

_____

HIGHLIGHT/BLUSH

_____

EYES

BROWS

_____

EYELID

_____

LINER

_____

CREASE

_____

MASCARA

_____

LIPS

LINER

_____

LIP COLOR

_____

GLOSS

_____

NOTES

NAME OF LOOK _____

EVENING ⭘
DAYTIME ⭘

FACE

MOISTURIZER

_____

CONCEALER

_____

FOUNDATION

_____

HIGHLIGHT/BLUSH

_____

EYES

BROWS

_____

EYELID

_____

LINER

_____

CREASE

_____

MASCARA

_____

LIPS

LINER

_____

LIP COLOR

_____

GLOSS

_____

NOTES

NAME OF LOOK _____

EVENING ○

DAYTIME ○

FACE

MOISTURIZER

_____

CONCEALER

_____

FOUNDATION

_____

HIGHLIGHT/BLUSH

_____

EYES

BROWS

_____

EYELID

_____

LINER

_____

CREASE

_____

MASCARA

LIPS

LINER

_____

LIP COLOR

_____

GLOSS

_____

NOTES

NAME OF LOOK _____

EVENING ○
DAYTIME ○

FACE

MOISTURIZER

_____

CONCEALER

_____

FOUNDATION

_____

HIGHLIGHT/BLUSH

_____

EYES

BROWS

_____

EYELID

_____

LINER

_____

CREASE

_____

MASCARA

_____

LIPS

LINER

_____

LIP COLOR

_____

GLOSS

_____

NOTES

NAME OF LOOK ⎯⎯⎯⎯⎯⎯⎯⎯

EVENING ◯
DAYTIME ◯

FACE

MOISTURIZER

⎯⎯⎯⎯⎯⎯⎯⎯⎯⎯

CONCEALER

⎯⎯⎯⎯⎯⎯⎯⎯⎯⎯

FOUNDATION

⎯⎯⎯⎯⎯⎯⎯⎯⎯⎯

HIGHLIGHT/BLUSH

⎯⎯⎯⎯⎯⎯⎯⎯⎯⎯

EYES

BROWS

⎯⎯⎯⎯⎯⎯⎯⎯⎯⎯

EYELID

⎯⎯⎯⎯⎯⎯⎯⎯⎯⎯

LINER

⎯⎯⎯⎯⎯⎯⎯⎯⎯⎯

CREASE

⎯⎯⎯⎯⎯⎯⎯⎯⎯⎯

MASCARA

⎯⎯⎯⎯⎯⎯⎯⎯⎯⎯

LIPS

LINER

⎯⎯⎯⎯⎯⎯⎯⎯⎯⎯

LIP COLOR

⎯⎯⎯⎯⎯⎯⎯⎯⎯⎯

GLOSS

⎯⎯⎯⎯⎯⎯⎯⎯⎯⎯

NOTES

NAME OF LOOK _____

EVENING ○
DAYTIME ○

FACE

MOISTURIZER

_____

CONCEALER

_____

FOUNDATION

_____

HIGHLIGHT/BLUSH

_____

EYES

BROWS

_____

EYELID

_____

LINER

_____

CREASE

_____

MASCARA

_____

LIPS

LINER

_____

LIP COLOR

_____

GLOSS

NOTES

NAME OF LOOK _____

EVENING ◯

DAYTIME ◯

FACE

MOISTURIZER

_____

CONCEALER

_____

FOUNDATION

_____

HIGHLIGHT/BLUSH

_____

EYES

BROWS

_____

EYELID

_____

LINER

_____

CREASE

_____

MASCARA

_____

LIPS

LINER

_____

LIP COLOR

_____

GLOSS

_____

NOTES

NAME OF LOOK _____

EVENING ◯

DAYTIME ◯

FACE

MOISTURIZER

_____

CONCEALER

_____

FOUNDATION

_____

HIGHLIGHT/BLUSH

_____

EYES

BROWS

_____

EYELID

_____

LINER

_____

CREASE

_____

MASCARA

_____

LIPS

LINER

_____

LIP COLOR

_____

GLOSS

_____

NOTES

NAME OF LOOK _____

EVENING ○
DAYTIME ○

FACE

MOISTURIZER

_____

CONCEALER

_____

FOUNDATION

_____

HIGHLIGHT/BLUSH

_____

EYES

BROWS

_____

EYELID

_____

LINER

_____

CREASE

_____

MASCARA

_____

LIPS

LINER

_____

LIP COLOR

_____

GLOSS

_____

NOTES

NAME OF LOOK _____

EVENING ○
DAYTIME ○

FACE

MOISTURIZER

_____

CONCEALER

_____

FOUNDATION

_____

HIGHLIGHT/BLUSH

_____

EYES

BROWS

_____

EYELID

_____

LINER

_____

CREASE

_____

MASCARA

_____

LIPS

LINER

_____

LIP COLOR

_____

GLOSS

_____

NOTES

NAME OF LOOK _____

EVENING ○

DAYTIME ○

FACE

MOISTURIZER

_____

CONCEALER

_____

FOUNDATION

_____

HIGHLIGHT/BLUSH

_____

EYES

BROWS

_____

EYELID

_____

LINER

_____

CREASE

_____

MASCARA

_____

LIPS

LINER

_____

LIP COLOR

_____

GLOSS

_____

NOTES

NAME OF LOOK _____

EVENING ○
DAYTIME ○

FACE

MOISTURIZER

_____

CONCEALER

_____

FOUNDATION

_____

HIGHLIGHT/BLUSH

_____

EYES

BROWS

_____

EYELID

_____

LINER

_____

CREASE

_____

MASCARA

_____

LIPS

LINER

_____

LIP COLOR

_____

GLOSS

_____

NOTES

NAME OF LOOK _____

EVENING ○

DAYTIME ○

FACE

MOISTURIZER

_____

CONCEALER

_____

FOUNDATION

_____

HIGHLIGHT/BLUSH

_____

EYES

BROWS

_____

EYELID

_____

LINER

_____

CREASE

_____

MASCARA

_____

LIPS

LINER

_____

LIP COLOR

_____

GLOSS

_____

NOTES

NAME OF LOOK _____

EVENING ⚪

DAYTIME ⚪

FACE

MOISTURIZER

_____

CONCEALER

_____

FOUNDATION

_____

HIGHLIGHT/BLUSH

_____

EYES

BROWS

_____

EYELID

_____

LINER

_____

CREASE

_____

MASCARA

LIPS

LINER

_____

LIP COLOR

_____

GLOSS

NOTES

NAME OF LOOK _____

EVENING ⚪

DAYTIME ⚪

FACE

MOISTURIZER

_____

CONCEALER

_____

FOUNDATION

_____

HIGHLIGHT/BLUSH

_____

EYES

BROWS

_____

EYELID

_____

LINER

_____

CREASE

_____

MASCARA

_____

LIPS

LINER

_____

LIP COLOR

_____

GLOSS

_____

NOTES

NAME OF LOOK _____

EVENING ○
DAYTIME ○

FACE

MOISTURIZER

_____

CONCEALER

_____

FOUNDATION

_____

HIGHLIGHT/BLUSH

_____

EYES

BROWS

_____

EYELID

_____

LINER

_____

CREASE

_____

MASCARA

_____

LIPS

LINER

_____

LIP COLOR

_____

GLOSS

_____

NOTES

NAME OF LOOK _____

EVENING ○
DAYTIME ○

FACE

MOISTURIZER
_____

CONCEALER
_____

FOUNDATION
_____

HIGHLIGHT/BLUSH
_____

EYES

BROWS
_____

EYELID
_____

LINER
_____

CREASE
_____

MASCARA
_____

LIPS

LINER
_____

LIP COLOR
_____

GLOSS
_____

NOTES

NAME OF LOOK _____

EVENING ○

DAYTIME ○

FACE

MOISTURIZER

_____

CONCEALER

_____

FOUNDATION

_____

HIGHLIGHT/BLUSH

_____

EYES

BROWS

_____

EYELID

_____

LINER

_____

CREASE

_____

MASCARA

LIPS

LINER

_____

LIP COLOR

_____

GLOSS

_____

NOTES

NAME OF LOOK _____

EVENING ○

DAYTIME ○

FACE

MOISTURIZER

_____

CONCEALER

_____

FOUNDATION

_____

HIGHLIGHT/BLUSH

_____

EYES

BROWS

_____

EYELID

_____

LINER

_____

CREASE

_____

MASCARA

_____

LIPS

LINER

_____

LIP COLOR

_____

GLOSS

_____

NOTES

NAME OF LOOK _____

EVENING ○

DAYTIME ○

FACE

MOISTURIZER

_____

CONCEALER

_____

FOUNDATION

_____

HIGHLIGHT/BLUSH

_____

EYES

BROWS

_____

EYELID

_____

LINER

_____

CREASE

_____

MASCARA

LIPS

LINER

_____

LIP COLOR

_____

GLOSS

_____

NOTES

NAME OF LOOK _____

EVENING ○

DAYTIME ○

FACE

MOISTURIZER

_____

CONCEALER

_____

FOUNDATION

_____

HIGHLIGHT/BLUSH

_____

EYES

BROWS

_____

EYELID

_____

LINER

_____

CREASE

_____

MASCARA

_____

LIPS

LINER

_____

LIP COLOR

_____

GLOSS

_____

NOTES

Name of Look _____

Evening ○

Daytime ○

Face

Moisturizer

_____

Concealer

_____

Foundation

_____

Highlight/Blush

_____

Eyes

Brows

_____

Eyelid

_____

Liner

_____

Crease

_____

Mascara

_____

Lips

Liner

_____

Lip Color

_____

Gloss

_____

Notes

NAME OF LOOK _____

EVENING ⚪

DAYTIME ⚪

FACE

MOISTURIZER

_____

CONCEALER

_____

FOUNDATION

_____

HIGHLIGHT/BLUSH

_____

EYES

BROWS

_____

EYELID

_____

LINER

_____

CREASE

_____

MASCARA

_____

LIPS

LINER

_____

LIP COLOR

_____

GLOSS

NOTES

NAME OF LOOK _____

EVENING ◯

DAYTIME ◯

FACE

MOISTURIZER

_____

CONCEALER

_____

FOUNDATION

_____

HIGHLIGHT/BLUSH

_____

EYES

BROWS

_____

EYELID

_____

LINER

_____

CREASE

_____

MASCARA

_____

LIPS

LINER

_____

LIP COLOR

_____

GLOSS

_____

NOTES

NAME OF LOOK _____

EVENING ○

DAYTIME ○

FACE

MOISTURIZER

_____

CONCEALER

_____

FOUNDATION

_____

HIGHLIGHT/BLUSH

_____

EYES

BROWS

_____

EYELID

_____

LINER

_____

CREASE

_____

MASCARA

_____

LIPS

LINER

_____

LIP COLOR

_____

GLOSS

_____

NOTES

NAME OF LOOK _____

EVENING ○

DAYTIME ○

FACE

MOISTURIZER

_____

CONCEALER

_____

FOUNDATION

_____

HIGHLIGHT/BLUSH

_____

EYES

BROWS

_____

EYELID

_____

LINER

_____

CREASE

_____

MASCARA

LIPS

LINER

_____

LIP COLOR

_____

GLOSS

NOTES

NAME OF LOOK _____

EVENING ○

DAYTIME ○

FACE

MOISTURIZER

_____

CONCEALER

_____

FOUNDATION

_____

HIGHLIGHT/BLUSH

_____

EYES

BROWS

_____

EYELID

_____

LINER

_____

CREASE

_____

MASCARA

_____

LIPS

LINER

_____

LIP COLOR

_____

GLOSS

_____

NOTES

NAME OF LOOK _____

EVENING ◯

DAYTIME ◯

FACE

MOISTURIZER

_____

CONCEALER

_____

FOUNDATION

_____

HIGHLIGHT/BLUSH

_____

EYES

BROWS

_____

EYELID

_____

LINER

_____

CREASE

_____

MASCARA

_____

LIPS

LINER

_____

LIP COLOR

_____

GLOSS

_____

NOTES

NAME OF LOOK _____

EVENING ○

DAYTIME ○

FACE

MOISTURIZER

_____

CONCEALER

_____

FOUNDATION

_____

HIGHLIGHT/BLUSH

_____

EYES

BROWS

_____

EYELID

_____

LINER

_____

CREASE

_____

MASCARA

LIPS

LINER

_____

LIP COLOR

_____

GLOSS

NOTES

NAME OF LOOK _____

EVENING ◯

DAYTIME ◯

FACE

MOISTURIZER
_____

CONCEALER
_____

FOUNDATION
_____

HIGHLIGHT/BLUSH
_____

EYES

BROWS
_____

EYELID
_____

LINER
_____

CREASE
_____

MASCARA
_____

LIPS

LINER
_____

LIP COLOR
_____

GLOSS
_____

NOTES

NAME OF LOOK _____

EVENING ⬤

DAYTIME ⬤

FACE

MOISTURIZER

_____

CONCEALER

_____

FOUNDATION

_____

HIGHLIGHT/BLUSH

_____

EYES

BROWS

_____

EYELID

_____

LINER

_____

CREASE

_____

MASCARA

_____

LIPS

LINER

_____

LIP COLOR

_____

GLOSS

_____

NOTES

NAME OF LOOK _____

EVENING ○

DAYTIME ○

FACE

MOISTURIZER

_____

CONCEALER

_____

FOUNDATION

_____

HIGHLIGHT/BLUSH

_____

EYES

BROWS

_____

EYELID

_____

LINER

_____

CREASE

_____

MASCARA

LIPS

LINER

_____

LIP COLOR

_____

GLOSS

_____

NOTES

NAME OF LOOK _____

EVENING ⚪

DAYTIME ⚪

FACE

MOISTURIZER

_____

CONCEALER

_____

FOUNDATION

_____

HIGHLIGHT/BLUSH

_____

EYES

BROWS

_____

EYELID

_____

LINER

_____

CREASE

_____

MASCARA

_____

LIPS

LINER

_____

LIP COLOR

_____

GLOSS

_____

NOTES

NAME OF LOOK _____

EVENING ○

DAYTIME ○

FACE

MOISTURIZER

_____

CONCEALER

_____

FOUNDATION

_____

HIGHLIGHT/BLUSH

_____

EYES

BROWS

_____

EYELID

_____

LINER

_____

CREASE

_____

MASCARA

LIPS

LINER

_____

LIP COLOR

_____

GLOSS

_____

NOTES

NAME OF LOOK _____

EVENING ○

DAYTIME ○

FACE

MOISTURIZER

_____

CONCEALER

_____

FOUNDATION

_____

HIGHLIGHT/BLUSH

_____

EYES

BROWS

_____

EYELID

_____

LINER

_____

CREASE

_____

MASCARA

_____

LIPS

LINER

_____

LIP COLOR

_____

GLOSS

_____

NOTES

NAME OF LOOK _____

EVENING ◯

DAYTIME ◯

FACE

MOISTURIZER

_____

CONCEALER

_____

FOUNDATION

_____

HIGHLIGHT/BLUSH

_____

EYES

BROWS

_____

EYELID

_____

LINER

_____

CREASE

_____

MASCARA

LIPS

LINER

_____

LIP COLOR

_____

GLOSS

_____

NOTES

NAME OF LOOK _____

EVENING ◯

DAYTIME ◯

FACE

MOISTURIZER

_____

CONCEALER

_____

FOUNDATION

_____

HIGHLIGHT/BLUSH

_____

EYES

BROWS

_____

EYELID

_____

LINER

_____

CREASE

_____

MASCARA

LIPS

LINER

_____

LIP COLOR

_____

GLOSS

NOTES

NAME OF LOOK _____

EVENING ○

DAYTIME ○

FACE

MOISTURIZER

_____

CONCEALER

_____

FOUNDATION

_____

HIGHLIGHT/BLUSH

_____

EYES

BROWS

_____

EYELID

_____

LINER

_____

CREASE

_____

MASCARA

_____

LIPS

LINER

_____

LIP COLOR

_____

GLOSS

_____

NOTES

NAME OF LOOK _____

EVENING ○

DAYTIME ○

FACE

MOISTURIZER

_____

CONCEALER

_____

FOUNDATION

_____

HIGHLIGHT/BLUSH

_____

EYES

BROWS

_____

EYELID

_____

LINER

_____

CREASE

_____

MASCARA

_____

LIPS

LINER

_____

LIP COLOR

_____

GLOSS

_____

NOTES

NAME OF LOOK _____

EVENING ◯

DAYTIME ◯

FACE

MOISTURIZER

_____

CONCEALER

_____

FOUNDATION

_____

HIGHLIGHT/BLUSH

_____

EYES

BROWS

_____

EYELID

_____

LINER

_____

CREASE

_____

MASCARA

LIPS

LINER

_____

LIP COLOR

_____

GLOSS

_____

NOTES

NAME OF LOOK _____

EVENING ○

DAYTIME ○

FACE

MOISTURIZER

_____

CONCEALER

_____

FOUNDATION

_____

HIGHLIGHT/BLUSH

_____

EYES

BROWS

_____

EYELID

_____

LINER

_____

CREASE

_____

MASCARA

_____

LIPS

LINER

_____

LIP COLOR

_____

GLOSS

_____

NOTES

NAME OF LOOK _____

EVENING ○
DAYTIME ○

FACE

MOISTURIZER

_____

CONCEALER

_____

FOUNDATION

_____

HIGHLIGHT/BLUSH

_____

EYES

BROWS

_____

EYELID

_____

LINER

_____

CREASE

_____

MASCARA

_____

LIPS

LINER

_____

LIP COLOR

_____

GLOSS

_____

NOTES

NAME OF LOOK _____

EVENING ⃝

DAYTIME ⃝

FACE

MOISTURIZER
_____

CONCEALER
_____

FOUNDATION
_____

HIGHLIGHT/BLUSH
_____

EYES

BROWS
_____

EYELID
_____

LINER
_____

CREASE
_____

MASCARA
_____

LIPS

LINER
_____

LIP COLOR
_____

GLOSS
_____

NOTES

NAME OF LOOK _____

EVENING ○
DAYTIME ○

FACE

MOISTURIZER
_____

CONCEALER
_____

FOUNDATION
_____

HIGHLIGHT/BLUSH
_____

EYES

BROWS
_____

EYELID
_____

LINER
_____

CREASE
_____

MASCARA

LIPS

LINER
_____

LIP COLOR
_____

GLOSS
_____

NOTES

NAME OF LOOK _____

EVENING ◯

DAYTIME ◯

FACE

MOISTURIZER

_____

CONCEALER

_____

FOUNDATION

_____

HIGHLIGHT/BLUSH

_____

EYES

BROWS

_____

EYELID

_____

LINER

_____

CREASE

_____

MASCARA

_____

LIPS

LINER

_____

LIP COLOR

_____

GLOSS

NOTES

NAME OF LOOK _____

EVENING ◯

DAYTIME ◯

FACE

MOISTURIZER

_____

CONCEALER

_____

FOUNDATION

_____

HIGHLIGHT/BLUSH

_____

EYES

BROWS

_____

EYELID

_____

LINER

_____

CREASE

_____

MASCARA

_____

LIPS

LINER

_____

LIP COLOR

_____

GLOSS

_____

NOTES

NAME OF LOOK _____

EVENING ○
DAYTIME ○

FACE

MOISTURIZER

_____

CONCEALER

_____

FOUNDATION

_____

HIGHLIGHT/BLUSH

_____

EYES

BROWS

_____

EYELID

_____

LINER

_____

CREASE

_____

MASCARA

LIPS

LINER

_____

LIP COLOR

_____

GLOSS

NOTES

NAME OF LOOK _____

EVENING ◯

DAYTIME ◯

FACE

MOISTURIZER

_____

CONCEALER

_____

FOUNDATION

_____

HIGHLIGHT/BLUSH

_____

EYES

BROWS

_____

EYELID

_____

LINER

_____

CREASE

_____

MASCARA

LIPS

LINER

_____

LIP COLOR

_____

GLOSS

_____

NOTES

NAME OF LOOK _____

EVENING ○

DAYTIME ○

FACE

MOISTURIZER

_____

CONCEALER

_____

FOUNDATION

_____

HIGHLIGHT/BLUSH

_____

EYES

BROWS

_____

EYELID

_____

LINER

_____

CREASE

_____

MASCARA

LIPS

LINER

_____

LIP COLOR

_____

GLOSS

NOTES

NAME OF LOOK _____

EVENING ⚪

DAYTIME ⚪

FACE

MOISTURIZER

_____

CONCEALER

_____

FOUNDATION

_____

HIGHLIGHT/BLUSH

_____

EYES

BROWS

_____

EYELID

_____

LINER

_____

CREASE

_____

MASCARA

_____

LIPS

LINER

_____

LIP COLOR

_____

GLOSS

_____

NOTES

NAME OF LOOK _____

EVENING ○
DAYTIME ○

FACE

MOISTURIZER

_____

CONCEALER

_____

FOUNDATION

_____

HIGHLIGHT/BLUSH

_____

EYES

BROWS

_____

EYELID

_____

LINER

_____

CREASE

_____

MASCARA

_____

LIPS

LINER

_____

LIP COLOR

_____

GLOSS

_____

NOTES

NAME OF LOOK _____

EVENING ◯

DAYTIME ◯

FACE

MOISTURIZER

_____

CONCEALER

_____

FOUNDATION

_____

HIGHLIGHT/BLUSH

_____

EYES

BROWS

_____

EYELID

_____

LINER

_____

CREASE

_____

MASCARA

_____

LIPS

LINER

_____

LIP COLOR

_____

GLOSS

_____

NOTES

NAME OF LOOK _____

EVENING ⚪

DAYTIME ⚪

FACE

MOISTURIZER

_____

CONCEALER

_____

FOUNDATION

_____

HIGHLIGHT/BLUSH

_____

EYES

BROWS

_____

EYELID

_____

LINER

_____

CREASE

_____

MASCARA

LIPS

LINER

_____

LIP COLOR

_____

GLOSS

_____

NOTES